COGNITIVE PSYCHOLGOY 2ND EDITION WORKBOOK

CONNOR WHITELEY

Copyright © 2020 CONNOR WHITELEY

All rights reserved.

DEDICATION
THANK YOU TO ALL MY READERS FOR THEIR CONTINUED SUPPORT, WITHOUT YOU I COULDN'T DO WHAT I LOVE.

QUESTIONS ABOUT MEMORY
What is the Multi-Store Model and how does it work?

....
....
....
....
....
....
....
....
....
....
....
....
....
....
....
....
....

Evaluate the Multi-Store Model.

What is the working model and how does it work?

COGNITIVE PSYCHOLGOY 2ND EDITION WORKBOOK

Evaluate the Working Model.

COGNITIVE PSYCHOLGOY 2ND EDITION WORKBOOK

COGNITIVE PSYCHOLGOY 2ND EDITION WORKBOOK

Discuss what is schema is and how does it impact our behaviour.

COGNITIVE PSYCHOLGOY 2ND EDITION WORKBOOK

What are flashbulb memories?

COGNITIVE PSYCHOLGOY 2ND EDITION WORKBOOK

Evaluate the reliability of memory.

Explain levels of processing theory

Explain how self-referencing can help with memory.

QUESTIONS ABOUT THINKING
What's thinking?

What's a Hereutics?

Explain the Framing Effect and the Peak-End Rule.

COGNITIVE PSYCHOLGOY 2ND EDITION WORKBOOK

Explain utility theory and it's evaluate.

Name a few things that can influence our thinking.

Discuss how neuroeconomics started.

Discuss the various biases that can influence our thinking.

COGNITIVE PSYCHOLGOY 2ND EDITION WORKBOOK

QUESTIONS ABOUT LEARNING
What's habituation?

Describe classical conditions

Describe operant condition

What's partial reinforcement?

What's a Ratio schedule?

What is positive reinforcement?

COGNITIVE PSYCHOLGOY 2ND EDITION WORKBOOK

What is negative reinforcement?

What is positive punishment?

What is negative punishment

QUESTIONS ABOUT SOCIAL COGNITION

Describe the following hypothesis for why humans have large brains:

Evolutionary

COGNITIVE PSYCHOLGOY 2ND EDITION WORKBOOK

Ecological hypothesis

COGNITIVE PSYCHOLGOY 2ND EDITION WORKBOOK

Social learning

COGNITIVE PSYCHOLGOY 2ND EDITION WORKBOOK

Discuss how mirror neurons are elated to empathy.

QUESTIONS ABOUT LANGUAGE
What is a language?

What is a phonemes and give three examples?

What is a morphemes?

How many morphemes are there in English?

Explain the definitional theory of word meaning.

Explain the prototype theory of meaning.

Discuss the different ways in which humans learn a language.

Explain the Whorfian hypothesis.

QUESTIONS ABOUT EMOTION
What 3 aspects do we define emotion in?

Explain the James-Lange Theory.

Explain Schacter's and Singer's theory.

According to Efren et al (1982) what 6 emotions are universal?

....
....
....
....
....
....
....
....
....
....
....
....
....
....
....
....
....
....
....
....
....
....
....
....
....
....
....
....

COGNITIVE PSYCHOLGOY 2ND EDITION WORKBOOK

https://www.subscribepage.com/psychologyboxset

Thank you for reading.

I hoped you enjoyed it.

If you want a FREE book and keep up to date about new books and project. Then please sign up for my newsletter at www.connorwhiteley.net/

Have a great day.

CHECK OUT THE PSYCHOLOGY WORLD PODCAST FOR MORE PSYCHOLOGY INFORMATION!

AVAILABLE ON ALL MAJOR PODCAST APPS.

About the author:

Connor Whiteley is the author of over 30 books in the sci-fi fantasy, nonfiction psychology and books for writer's genre and he is a Human Branding Speaker and Consultant.

He is a passionate warhammer 40,000 reader, psychology student and author.

Who narrates his own audiobooks and he hosts The Psychology World Podcast.

All whilst studying Psychology at the University of Kent, England.

Also, he was a former Explorer Scout where he gave a speech to the Maltese President in August 2018 and he attended Prince Charles' 70th Birthday Party at Buckingham Palace in May 2018.

Plus, he is a self-confessed coffee lover!

Please follow me on:

Website: www.connorwhiteley.net

Twitter: @scifiwhiteley

Please leave on honest review as this helps with the discoverability of the book and I truly appreciate it.

Thank you for reading. I hope you've enjoyed.

COGNITIVE PSYCHOLGOY 2ND EDITION WORKBOOK

All books in 'An Introductory Series':

BIOLOGICAL PSYCHOLOGY 3RD EDITION

COGNITIVE PSYCHOLOGY 2ND EDITION

SOCIAL PSYCHOLOGY- 3RD EDITION

ABNORMAL PSYCHOLOGY 3RD EDITION

PSYCHOLOGY OF RELATIONSHIPS- 3RD EDITION

DEVELOPMENTAL PSYCHOLOGY 3RD EDITION

HEALTH PSYCHOLOGY

RESEARCH IN PSYCHOLOGY

A GUIDE TO MENTAL HEALTH AND TREATMENT AROUND THE WORLD- A GLOBAL LOOK AT DEPRESSION

FORENSIC PSYCHOLOGY

CLINICAL PSYCHOLOGY

FORMULATION IN PSYCHOTHERAPY

Other books by Connor Whiteley:

THE ANGEL OF RETURN

THE ANGEL OF FREEDOM

GARRO: GALAXY'S END

GARRO: RISE OF THE ORDER

GARRO: END TIMES

GARRO: SHORT STORIES

GARRO: COLLECTION

GARRO: HERESY

GARRO: FAITHLESS

GARRO: DESTROYER OF WORLDS

GARRO: COLLECTIONS BOOK 4-6

GARRO: MISTRESS OF BLOOD

GARRO: BEACON OF HOPE

GARRO: END OF DAYS

WINTER'S COMING

WINTER'S HUNT

COGNITIVE PSYCHOLGOY 2ND EDITION WORKBOOK

WINTER'S REVENGE

WINTER'S DISSENSION

Companion guides:

BIOLOGICAL PSYCHOLOGY 2ND EDITION WORKBOOK

COGNITIVE PSYCHOLOGY 2ND EDITION WORKBOOK

SOCIOCULTURAL PSYCHOLOGY 2ND EDITION WORKBOOK

ABNORMAL PSYCHOLOGY 2ND EDITION WORKBOOK

PSYCHOLOGY OF HUMAN RELATIONSHIPS 2ND EDITION WORKBOOK

HEALTH PSYCHOLOGY WORKBOOK

FORENSIC PSYCHOLOGY WORKBOOK

Audiobooks by Connor Whiteley:

BIOLOGICAL PSYCHOLOGY

COGNITIVE PSYCHOLOGY

SOCIOCULTURAL PSYCHOLOGY

ABNORMAL PSYCHOLOGY

PSYCHOLOGY OF HUMAN RELATIONSHIPS

HEALTH PSYCHOLOGY

DEVELOPMENTAL PSYCHOLOGY

RESEARCH IN PSYCHOLOGY

FORENSIC PSYCHOLOGY

GARRO: GALAXY'S END

GARRO: RISE OF THE ORDER

GARRO: SHORT STORIES

GARRO: END TIMES

GARRO: COLLECTION

GARRO: HERESY

GARRO: FAITHLESS

GARRO: DESTROYER OF WORLDS

GARRO: COLLECTION BOOKS 4-6

GARRO: COLLECTION BOOKS 1-6

Business books:

TIME MANAGEMENT: A GUIDE FOR STUDENTS AND WORKERS

LEADERSHIP: WHAT MAKES A GOOD LEADER? A GUIDE FOR STUDENTS AND WORKERS.

BUSINESS SKILLS: HOW TO SURVIVE THE BUSINESS WORLD? A GUIDE FOR STUDENTS, EMPLOYEES AND EMPLOYERS.

BUSINESS COLLECTION

GET YOUR FREE BOOK AT:
WWW.CONNORWHITELEY.NET

www.ingramcontent.com/pod-product-compliance
Lightning Source LLC
LaVergne TN
LVHW011840060526
838200LV00054B/4117